EXTREME IRONING

EXTREME IRONING

PHIL SHAW

NEW
HOLLAND

First published in 2003 by
New Holland Publishers (UK) Ltd
London • Cape Town • Sydney • Auckland
www.newhollandpublishers.com

Garfield House
86–88 Edgware Road
London W2 2EA
United Kingdom

80 McKenzie Street
Cape Town 8001
South Africa

Level 1, Unit 4
Suite 411, 14 Aquatic Drive
Frenchs Forest,NSW 2086
Australia

218 Lake Road
Northcote, Auckland
New Zealand

10 9 8 7 6 5 4 3 2 1

ISBN 1 84330 555 0

Editorial Assistance: Penny Wilkinson
Editor: Gareth Jones
Editorial Direction: Rosemary Wilkinson
Designer: Paul Wright
Photographers: See page 96

Reproduction by Modern Age Repro House Ltd,
Hong Kong
Printed and bound by Star Standard Industries Pte Ltd,
Singapore.

DISCLAIMER
**Participating in any extreme or adventure sport is
potentially dangerous. All activities are undertaken at
your own risk. The Extreme Ironing Bureau and the
Publisher accept no responsibility for accidents or
injury caused by or resulting from participation in the
sports covered in this book.**

There is a small group of people who will travel to the very ends of the Earth in search of new challenges. They will risk everything for the experience of adventure and danger. For them, nature itself is not enough of a challenge. These people are extreme ironists.

Extreme ironing is the latest adrenaline sport – combining the thrills of outdoor activity with the satisfaction of a well-pressed shirt.

Most ironists love the thrill of combining the everyday with the exciting. Ask a mountaineer why he or she climbs, they often answer, "Because it's there." An extreme ironist irons his or her clothes, "Because they're creased."

Over the years I tried my hand at a number of so-called extreme sports. Rock climbing, scuba diving, surfing, abseiling, caving and mountain biking – I tried them all. But in each case I was left wanting that little bit extra. I found what I was looking for in extreme ironing.

It is fair to say that the sport is now a global phenomenon with sports men and women from some 20 countries taking ironing to the edge and beyond. The sport has come on a long way since its birth in the city of Leicester, England, in 1997. There are now regular events, competitions and a number of websites dedicated to the sport. September 2002 saw the first World Championships with 80 competitors from 10 countries going iron-to-iron in extreme outdoor conditions.

This book has been written as a complete guide to everything you'll ever need to know about the world's first white goods extreme

sport. For newcomers, the basics of extreme ironing are explained with attention paid to all aspects, from choosing your iron to selecting your fabric. Later on, the different styles of extreme ironing are described and, in the final section of the book, competitive extreme ironing is explored.

Extreme ironing has given me a great deal of satisfaction over the years. To me, there's no other sport that matches it for excitement, danger or skill. Next time you are ironing your shirt for work on a Sunday evening, just think, you could have taken it outside and joined the latest sporting craze: extreme ironing.

Iron on!
Steam
April 2003

Taking ironing to the edge

PART ONE: AN INTRODUCTION TO EXTREME IRONING

HOW IT ALL BEGAN...

The English East Midlands city of Leicester has never been known as a place of excitement or danger, in fact it's often thought of as a little boring. Yet in 1997, against these odds, the city gave birth to extreme ironing.

Returning home late one afternoon, after a long day in the knitwear factory, the sun shining and a balmy breeze blowing my way, the last thing I wanted to do was start on a pile of ironing. I much preferred the idea of an evening out pursuing my (somewhat unsuccessful) hobby of rock climbing... And so, I got out my extension lead. When my housemate Paul returned home from work, he found me ironing in the back garden – practising a few moves. He asked what I was doing. "Extreme ironing," was my stoic reply, and a new sport was born. I soon realised that this new sport might seem strange to some people, so Paul and I adopted the pseudonyms Spray and Steam in order to avoid the ridicule of our peers.

We practised moves in our pokey back garden, then recruited a number of additional members including Starch, Basket, Short Fuse, Flex and Fe, and formed the Extreme Ironing Bureau to promote the development of the sport.

In the beginning...

Despite the initial success of extreme ironing in North Wales and England's Lake District, general take-up of the sport was slow. The EIB moved underground to avoid a backlash from participants of other so-called extreme sports such as rock climbing, canoeing and sky-diving. Fellow founder member Spray found himself "experimenting" with other extreme activities, most notably extreme hair-styling, so sadly we went our separate ways.

In mid-June 1999, I embarked on a worldwide recruitment campaign with Short Fuse. Armed only with a training iron, we toured America, Fiji, New Zealand, Australia and Southern Africa. A chance meeting in New Zealand with a creased party of thrill-seeking Germans, who were very excited about the possibilities of extreme ironing, led to the next stage of EIB's development – Extreme Ironing International. The following year a team of determined and enthusiastic Germans, led by Hot Crease, set up a sister office – the German Extreme Ironing

Starch – one of the original ironists

Steam stops for a breather in the Scottish Highlands

Hotwire dutifully performs the role of board for Steam

Section (GEIS), which has been at the forefront of developments ever since, including the organisation of the first ever Extreme Ironing World Championships in 2002.

Back in the UK, extreme ironing regained its popularity, and with a hardcore group of ironists led by Starch, Basket and myself, the sport expanded exponentially.

There never seems to be a shortage of newcomers, happy to drop the boring "household-chore" image of ironing and take it outside, under the sky, where it belongs.

EXTREME IRONING DEFINED

**extreme ironing / ɪkˈstrːm ˈʌɪənɪŋ / n.
sport involving ironing clothes outdoors in
dangerous or unusual locations
[origin Leicester, 1997].**

Extreme ironing requires participants to iron
items of laundry in remote, inhospitable,
dangerous or unusual locations. It usually
combines the discipline of another extreme
sport such as rock climbing, mountaineering,
canoeing, scuba diving or surfing, with the
mundane task of domestic ironing.

Participants of the sport are known as ironists
and pride themselves on returning to work on a
Monday morning with a well-ironed shirt, which
they pressed at the weekend whilst dangling
from a rock face or riding the rapids.

The climb is only half the challenge

Shark-infested waters? No problem for Basket

GETTING STARTED

For safety reasons the EIB recommends that newcomers should start off ironing in a safe environment such as a garden or local park, before moving on to more extreme locations. Irons can be hot and we don't want people getting burnt! Once well-practised at the novice moves, ironists can move on to combine ironing with other extreme sports such as rock climbing or surfing, where the added technical difficulty of handling a hot iron and wrinkled fabrics tests even the most daring sportspeople. Rock climbing, for example, is difficult enough without strapping an ironing board to your back and having a hot iron dangling from your harness.

Difficulty level: Easy

It's all about balance

Start on the ground

With a little help from my friends

Smell the sea breeze

Iron in its natural setting

SELECTING YOUR IRON

When an athlete mentions his number one iron, you would be forgiven for assuming he or she was a golfer. But they could well be an extreme ironist. The iron is the principal piece of equipment – as important to an ironist as a racket to a tennis player or a foil to a fencer.

- **One iron** – Heavy weight "professional" iron, usually 1,800–2,000W. Excellent for those stubborn creases and strenuous situations involving high winds but too heavy and awkward for long distance ironing. Not suitable for a novice ironist.

- **Two iron** – A good all-round tool, though not as effective on stubborn creases as the one iron. Medium weight, usually around 1,600W.

- **Three iron** – Light weight "training" iron. Light enough to slip into a rucksack for spontaneous extreme ironing. Usually lacking in advanced features such as self-clean.

- **Four iron** – Ultra-light weight "travel" iron. Carry it with you for "anytime, anywhere" extreme ironing. Quality is compromised for the sake of portability.

POWERING YOUR IRON

For non-ironists, powering the iron is one of extreme ironing's biggest mysteries and usually subject to their scrutiny. A common comment is: "I bet you need long extension cords!" The suggestion is not as far from the truth as you might expect. In a competitive environment, where consistent power is a priority, irons are charged up at a nearby power source before being used on the fabric. A number one iron (around 1,800 watts) usually has enough heat in it to manage a shirt, and the challenge is to finish the garment before the iron is cold. The requirement for really "extreme" ironing in remote locations has led to the development of other methods of powering the iron. In the UK, Starch and Hotplate have been investigating the use of battery- and gas-powered irons, but it's early days for these. In Germany, Doctor Iron Q has developed the DSS Sorption System. This involves a specially modified iron that has a patented chemical formula inserted into the soleplate, which heats up when water is applied – perfect for remote extreme ironing.

"Getting the right heat is as important for extreme ironing as it is for domestic ironing," advises Iron Matron. "Too cold, and you won't get those stubborn creases out. Too hot and the fabric will pucker up, or, worse still, burn through. And, in a competitive situation, you'll lose points for any of these."

Ironing Border makes use of an alternative board

THE IMPORTANCE OF YOUR BOARD

No matter how good your iron is, without an ironing board, trying to get a crease out of a garment is almost impossible – particularly in an extreme environment. In the past, some ironists have been known to improvise – using a miniature ironing board or even an inverted surf- or snowboard. Whilst this practice is okay, there's no substituting the thrill of getting a full-size ironing board into an inhospitable environment such as the bottom of a lake, a sheer cliff-face or the cramped interior of a cave, opening it and beginning to iron. Starch explains the importance of the board: "When Iron Man Stumpy and I went to the Aiguillette d'Argentière near Chamonix in the French Alps to train for the world championships, we managed to forget our ironing board and had to use the one from the hotel. Unfortunately it was made from solid, one-inch thick wood and was very cumbersome, not at all ideal for hanging off a rock-face. That's the last time we make that mistake, I can tell you."

Hanging off the water tower

"Always start with the sleeves," recommends the EIB

CHOOSING YOUR FABRIC

One aspect of extreme ironing that is often overlooked is the garment to be ironed. Ironists are sometimes so absorbed in getting themselves into some sort of awkward or dangerous situation with their ironing board that they forget the main reason they are there in the first place: to rid their clothing of creases and wrinkles.

Any garment is perfectly suitable for extreme ironing. However, always check the "laundry care" label first both to make sure it's suitable for ironing and also what heat to apply.

According to a survey of ironists, the most popular choice of garment is a shirt (29%) – probably due to its technical difficulty – followed by boxer shorts (14%) and tea-towel (11%) – the novice's favourite. Trousers are apparently the least popular, winning favour with only 5% of ironists.

Putting the garment first

SAFETY FIRST

As with all extreme sports there is a certain amount of danger involved with extreme ironing. However, this is no excuse for not taking full safety precautions. We always advise ironists to iron within their limitations and approach extreme ironing as they would any other extreme sport. Always check your equipment before venturing out and never mix electricity and water. Extreme ironing should never be done alone. The EIB does not encourage "solo extreme ironing" – always use the "buddy system".

Despite all the best intentions, things don't always go according to plan. An Austrian extreme ironist, FoitnBegler, explains how a trip to a local waterfall resulted in a number of losses: "A short moment of carelessness in the rapidly flowing water and the current took the ironing board and swallowed it," he says. "We also nearly lost a team mate! It proved to be a costly day with our losses including one digital camera, one ironing board and all of our well-pressed laundry!"

Safety first for Australian, Jeremy Irons

FoitnBegler now takes the right precautions

Extreme ironing from another perspective

PART TWO: IRONING STYLES

OVERVIEW

After the initial step of taking ironing out of the house and into the garden, the first place we really tested our new-found extreme ironing skills was in the mountains of the Snowdonia region in Wales. Here, the barren, rugged landscape seemed somehow in keeping with the spirit of the sport.

Although the initial take-up of the sport was amongst the rock climbing fraternity, it soon became abundantly clear that the scope of extreme ironing was far broader than just Rocky-style. The sport steamed on into new areas as varied as Forest-style, Water-style, Urban-style and Freestyle.

In this next section, we explore these different categories, offering hot tips and rating the styles according to popularity and difficulty.

FOREST-STYLE

At its most basic level, Forest-style involves ironing on the ground in a forest. Daring ironists like nothing more than to take their irons, boards and laundry high into the treetops and uncrease their fabrics in the upper-most branches. Whether ironing in tropical Brazilian rainforest, the dense Black Forest of Southern Germany or the Australian bush, combining the thrill of extreme ironing with a sense of being at one with nature is an unequalled experience. Because of this association with their natural environment, Forest-style ironists are often labelled "hippie-ironists" or "tree pressers".

The privacy of a secluded forest attracts many ironists who are uncomfortable with the attention that the sport receives. Forest-style is recommended to beginners as a good place to start extreme ironing, when they are ready to branch out from the safety of the back garden.

Hot Pants shows no fear in the tree tops
of the Black Forest

IronNori branches out

"I've always seen Forest-style as the most unique extreme ironing style," says nature lover, Short-Fuse. "How many extreme sports do you know that you take part in 20 metres up a tree? It can be quite a challenge too, especially trying to get your ironing board in between the branches."

Tips: Find stable branches to rest your open board on. Always use ropes and harnesses when climbing tall trees. Always respect the environment. Don't damage trees.

Popularity: ••
Difficulty level: Easy–Moderate

Don't get out the wrong side!

WATER-STYLE

Sceptics often wonder about the validity of extreme ironing in the water, but it is very easy to forget the fact that moisture is an integral part of domestic ironing, usually facilitated through the spray function. Water-style extreme ironists like to take it one step further, with lots of water.

The first recorded instance of Water-style extreme ironing was in a Bavarian lake in Southern Germany. Ignoring the ice-cold water, the German ironists pressed on and discovered the exhilaration of ironing in these conditions. It wasn't long before Iron Lung took Water-style to the next level, combining it with scuba diving for the ultimate aquatic ironing thrill. Other variations of Water-style involve a blend of ironing and canoeing or surfing, and simply ironing in rivers.

FoitnBegler almost lost a member in the water

IronNori describes the first time the Austrian Section got involved in Water-style: "Sunday afternoon and we felt like ironing. The weather was good and it didn't take much time to pick up some friends and equipment. The Kaiser Gorge looked like the perfect location for an extreme ironing session. It's incredible but true – you can iron under or in water. It's a bit more difficult, but definitely possible." What couldn't be shown in this photo (previous page) is that the water temperature was well below 10°C and dangerously fast flowing. "If the session had lasted a minute more, our team would have lost a member!"

Popularity: •••
Difficulty level: Tricky

Note: For safety reasons, do not use electric irons for Water-style extreme ironing.

A good spray helps remove creases

Iron Matron and Travel Iron share a joke

Blonde ironists have more fun

Just enough air to finish this shirt

WATER-STYLE – UNDERWATER IRONING

Underwater ironing, devised by Iron Lung, takes ironing to the depths of ocean or lake, and usually requires scuba-diving equipment. Beginners can start by going just a few feet underwater, using snorkelling equipment.

Iron Lung offers good advice on first trying Underwater ironing: "It is very important to protect yourself from the cold. A neoprene suit is vital for underwater ironing. To maintain neutral buoyancy, ironists must take the weight of the iron and board into consideration and deduct this from the weights worn on the belt. It is also best to take easy-to-iron garments – T-shirts rather than trousers – to minimise ironing time. When ironing at depth (30 metres plus) you mustn't exceed the calculated ironing time. Plan your iron and iron your plan!"

Popularity: ••••
Difficulty level: Extreme

Ironing with the fishes

Iron-Lung takes extreme ironing to new depths

Preparing the ironing zone

A drysuit is essential

WATER-STYLE – UNDER-ICE IRONING

Since 1997, extreme ironing has taken place on water, in water, under water and on ice, but never before *beneath* the ice. Ironist Siltkicker bravely took his board and iron below frozen waters in North Wisconsin, USA and ironed below 40 cm of ice.

Siltkicker reports: "My project was to saw a hole in the ice, scuba dive under it with the appropriate gear, harness, and surface support team, and iron my shirt on the ice sheet above me. The iron was a Black & Decker Quick 'n' Easy 410, and the board was a wooden frame around which the shirt was buttoned. After arriving at the quarry we cleared the ice of snow and commenced sawing an iron-shaped hole with a chainsaw.

"Equipment included a vulcanised rubber drysuit and gloves, thermal undergarments, buoyancy compensator with tank and "pony"

Just enough light to iron by

Unfortunately, after ironing, the shirt froze

(emergency bail-out) bottle, harness and line, mask and fins, shears for cutting away any entanglements, compass, hoses and gauges, and 22 pounds of lead shot," adds Siltkicker.

"Once in the hole I placed a purpose-built frame, with the shirt around it, against the lower surface of the ice and commenced ironing. It was a beautiful, almost poetic experience and I felt at one with nature. Just me and the confused trout. Visibility underwater was crystal clear - you could see about a hundred feet.

"With under-ice ironing, it's important to get the garment on a hanger quickly after ironing. Due to the rapid formation of ice crystals, the shirt freezes in seconds," continues Siltkicker. "If you are quick enough you can stretch it into shape properly. I wasn't!"

Popularity: •
Difficulty level: Extreme

URBAN-STYLE

Many non-ironists think the difficulty of Urban-style lies in the "extreme embarrassment" of ironing on the street in front of large crowds. This is a misconception – Urban-style can be as demanding and skilful as any of the other styles of extreme ironing.

Borrowing moves from the skateboarding and roller-blading fraternity, devotees of this brand of extreme ironing have catapulted the sport into a new dimension.

Tips: Keep it legal, no trespassing and no damaging property.

Popularity: •••
Difficulty level: Moderate

It's anything but pedestrian

Ironist combines surf skills with Urban-style

Germany's Iron Mike flies into his laundry

FREESTYLE

Gymnastic, graceful and often beautiful to watch, Freestyle embraces freedom of movement, imagination and artistic expression. As its name suggests, in Freestyle anything goes, and it is the only style of extreme ironing in which ironists often work together as a team. If you are lucky enough to see a group of sportsmen and women creating a human pyramid, balancing an ironing board at the top and pressing their garment, you will be watching Freestyle ironists. Synchronised swimming, trampolining and ice skating all form part of the Freestyle family.

Tips: Always warm up and stretch properly before attempting difficult moves. Practise with a cold iron first and perfect your moves, before trying them with heat.

Popularity: ••
Difficulty level: Moderate

Hot Pants gets on her bike

ROCKY-STYLE

The king of extreme ironing is Rocky-style. In a recent survey carried out by the Extreme Ironing Bureau, Rocky-style was voted as the most popular form of extreme ironing, with 30% of respondents preferring it to all other styles. Many purists argue that it's the only true form of extreme ironing, as it requires high levels of skill and nerves of steel. The most common form of Rocky-style involves climbing mountains or sheer cliff-faces and ironing at the summit. Other versions of Rocky-style include Downhill (extreme ironing while skiing or snowboarding) and a brand new form – Underground extreme ironing.

Tips: Always monitor the weather. An ironing board strapped to the back acts like a sail in high winds. Wind is good for drying laundry but we don't want people being blown away.

Popularity: •••••
Difficulty: Extreme

A tricky move for Hotplate

Basket descends after a difficult route

ROCKY-STYLE (continued)

Extreme ironists the world over marvelled at the awesome achievements of a group of London-based ironists who decided to rid their tea-towels of creases in the French Alps.

Team spokesman Father P takes time out to describe the day in the Alps: "The site we selected was the Aiguillette d'Argentière, an impressive spike of rock at about 1,800 metres, sticking out of the side of the Aiguilles Rouges in the Chamonix Valley. When we reconnoitred the area the day before, it was sunny and we expected a good day's extreme ironing, but when we returned the weather wasn't so good. We reached the summit at 14.30 in the driving rain, after a two-hour ascent from Camp One. We certainly didn't need the spray function of our iron!

"Ironing was carried out by our lead ironist, Iron Man Stumpy – first across a yawning chasm, then at the summit. Sadly the

Ironing between a rock and a hard place

achievement was marred by damage sustained by the iron during the descent, when it appeared to come adrift and swung wildly into the cliff face, taking a savage blow to the handle. This was a stern reminder of the dangers of this exciting sport."

The pinnacle of extreme ironing

Rock climber, turned ironist, Ironside says, "Rocky-style is like vertical chess. An almost infinite number of moves on the climb, before getting to the end-game – ironing at the top. Checkmate!"

Short Fuse ready to catch Steam

ROCKY-STYLE: TECHNIQUES

More than with any other type of extreme ironing, successful Rocky-style depends upon teamwork. Climbing involves a "leader" and "seconder".

The lead climber sets off first, usually taking the iron with them – fastened to their harness for safety. During the climb, the leader puts their "protection" – essential items such as wires and camming devices – into the placements with their fall protected by the "belayer" on the rope.

Experienced leaders will sometimes take the board, but it usually falls to the seconder to fasten it to their back and carry it up. It is very important to keep the board central on the back in order to maintain a balanced centre-of-gravity. Once at the top of the climb, all that remains is to power up the iron and rid those garments of unsightly wrinkles. As Redhotwedge says, "Remember, always iron safely, and live to iron another day. That pile of laundry ain't gonna go away in a hurry, so don't take risks with it."

Preaching to the inverted

"Get that board over here Hotplate," says Starch

Short Fuse keeps Fe on the straight and narrow

ROCKY-STYLE: DOWNHILL

Big mountains, the fresh air, lots of snow, boards and skis – it's easy to see the attraction of Downhill Rocky-style. In some ways this version of extreme ironing is the complete antithesis of traditional Rocky-style, as the ironists complete their ironing on the way down from the top of a mountain.

Extreme ironing first went ski- and snowboard-crazy in the French Three Valleys ski area in March 2001. It was during that historic month that ironists Cool Silk, Fe, Safety Setting, Hotwire, Powercord and Hotplate first adopted their pseudonyms and extreme ironed for the first time, revelling in the harsh snowy conditions. Fuelled by the thrill of extreme ironing, these daring ironists performed an exhibition show at the bottom of the Grand Bosses ski run at Courchevel, much to the surprise and bemusement of the French skiers and snowboarders looking on.

Fe and Steam 'boarding'

Making good use of a nasty fall

In Downhill Rocky-style circles a debate rages on between snowboarders and skiers: the advantages of having a makeshift board to hand and the potential for acrobatics versus the speed of ironing whilst skiing. Both camps, however, agree on the challenges it offers.

Safety Setting, top après-ski ironist, explains why he loves it: "If there's one thing better than skiing on good powder, it's ironing on good powder. I've been combining my love of skiing and ironing for three years now and there's no greater thrill than getting a crisp white shirt on crisp white snow."

Tips: Be careful getting on and off the chairlifts, a back-mounted ironing board sometimes makes it easier. An inverted snowboard makes a good makeshift ironing board.

Popularity: •••
Difficulty level: Tricky

There's no business like snowbusiness

UNDERGROUND-STYLE

Underground-style is the latest version of extreme ironing. The first ever case was recorded in Castleton, a popular area for caving in the north of England. The main difficulty of this particular style lies in trying to get the bulky equipment through tight gaps and narrow tunnels, and into the furthest recesses of the cave.

As with a number of other extreme ironing specializations, Underground-style ironists employ a range of dedicated equipment for extreme ironing. The basics usually include an over-suit made of a tough material (usually Cordura or PVC) and an under-suit for warmth. Wellington boots, knee pads, a caving helmet, rubber gloves (for grip), lighting system and belts are other essentials. Items such as ropes, climbing gear or even diving equipment can be used to tackle particular obstacles within some caves.

Taking ironing underground

"If you think getting an iron up a mountain or balanced on a canoe is difficult, you should try Underground-style extreme ironing," says caver, Ironic. "I challenge any climber or canoeist to try their hand at it. Getting the board through the tightest cracks in dark, cold conditions many many metres underground is only for the dedicated ironist."

Tips: Relax when squeezing through small holes. Ironing purists may prefer to cover their board to avoid dirtying the garment during ironing.

Popularity: ••
Difficulty level: Moderate

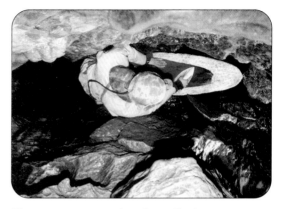

Please ensure your iron is earthed

Getting the garment out clean is a challenge

Remember to let go of that iron, Tirony!

IRON HURLING

The origins of iron hurling date back to 1800BC and the Tailteann Games in Ireland – 1,000 years before any record of the ancient Olympic Games. Along with other track and field events, athletes tied pieces of iron to ropes and competed to see who could hurl the piece of iron the longest distance. This iron became a hammer, made its way into the Olympics, and the sport is still being played today. In 1997, the original form of iron hurling was reborn when we took an iron on to the Welsh mountains in order to find out who could hurl it the furthest.

In 2002, this unique variation of extreme ironing was formalised with a set of rules, and the objective of participants throwing their iron a distance of around 50 metres into a set of rings (receiving more points the closer to the centre their iron lands). It is best played on a remote sandy beach, as damage to the iron is minimal and there is less chance of accidentally hitting a bystander.

Tips: Best played with a medium weight iron, number one irons are a bit too heavy to get any distance and a number four travel iron is too light for accuracy.

Popularity: ••
Difficulty level: Moderate

Steam about to let rip

ESO-IRONING

Eso-Ironing was invented in Germany as a way of improving health and mental wellbeing by combining outdoor ironing with meditation.

The German extreme ironing website, www.extremeironing.de, reveals that the discipline is based on the ancient and powerful discipline of Yoga: "This type of extreme ironing involves synchronising the breath with a progressive series of postures while ironing. The external heat stimulates the production of intense internal heat, and a purifying sweat that detoxifies muscles and organs. The result is improved circulation, a light and strong body, a calm mind and tidy clothes."

According to participants, Eso-Ironing is an effective technique for eliminating stress, increasing creativity and intelligence, and attaining inner happiness and fulfilment. Through applying the core elements of Eso-Ironing – heat, water, movement and

The Eso-ironing guru

pressure – practitioners claim to connect their Chakras (subtle energy centres located around the Etheric body or aura) with their physical body. Suffice to say that many extreme ironists are sceptical about the benefits of Eso-Ironing.

Popularity: •
Difficulty level: Moderate

It makes you flexible...

...and gives you perfect balance

The ironist in front is...

PART THREE:
LEADING NATIONS

LEADING EXTREME IRONING NATIONS

Following the introduction of the sport in Great Britain, extreme ironing spread to Germany in 2000. Since then, it has grown exponentially, and it is now estimated that outbreaks of extreme ironing have been recorded in some 20 countries including Australia, Austria, Chile, Croatia, Japan, New Zealand, South Africa and the United States of America.

As I have watched the take-up of extreme ironing through the creases and folds of Europe and beyond, I have noticed that different countries demonstrate different strengths, skills and abilities. For example, the Austrians have to be some of the best Rocky-style ironists I have seen, whereas the Australians are undoubtedly the masters of the water.

Basket goes off-piste

Ironing in one breath

AUSTRALIA

Australian ironists relate well to their natural environment, making good use of warm coastal waters and the wilderness of the Outback.

In Water-style, the Aussies have been breaking new ground, holding the first extreme ironing competition outside Europe. Through a leading Australian scuba diving website, ironists were challenged to send in their best underwater extreme ironing pictures, with the winner receiving a prize of $1,000. The take-up of the competition was so high that a dive company at Palm Beach, Sydney even offered a discount for those interested in ironing under water.

Elsewhere in 2002, a group of Australian ironists took their iron and board to the wilds of Yorke Peninsular on the south coast. Fastening the board to a sheet of corrugated iron and attaching it to the back of a truck, the madcap ironists were able to iron at speed. It was good to see that they had the sense to wear a helmet while ironing, but it is still not a style we would necessarily endorse.

Ironists to watch: Fabulon, Jeremy Irons.

Jeremy Irons and his specially modifed bike

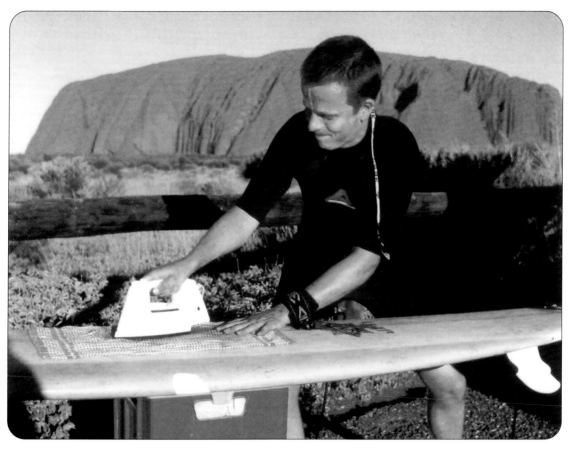

Ironing Boarder seems somehow out of place

AUSTRIA

The common belief of the majority of ironists is that one day Austria will dominate the sport. You only have to visit the Austrian extreme ironing website, www.ironing.at, to see how well extreme ironing can be done. Asked what their favourite style of extreme ironing was, team captain FoitnBegler says: "We are from Tyrol in the Alps and we like the mountains. We also enjoy ironing in the trees – anything up!"

Austrian ironists are utterly fearless, enjoy ironing at altitude and are pretty good in the water as well. If they have one weakness it would be in their ironing skills: they usually get themselves into such scrapes that their freshly pressed laundry often takes second place.

Ironists to watch: All of them, particularly FoitnBegler, IronNori and Rock the Iron.

FoitnBegler ironing on Cloud Nine

CHILE

There is only one registered ironist from Chile. His name is IronPablo and he is very proud that he is able to represent his nation at the highest level. His main aim is to make extreme ironing as popular in Chile as it is in Europe.

As a geologist, IronPablo is particularly interested in using the earth's natural energy supply to power his iron. German scientist, Doctor Iron Q, has been studying the use of "geo-thermics" for some time. If either Doctor Iron Q or IronPablo get it working they could hold an unnatural advantage over the rest of the competition.

Ironists to watch: Just IronPablo at the moment.

IronPablo – the hope of a nation

CROATIA

The popularity of extreme ironing in Germany has spilled over into nearby Croatia. The sport is still relatively unknown in Croatia, compared to countries like Austria and Great Britain, but a patriotic team wearing Croatian football strips are furiously plugging away.

The team, known collectively as "Elnog" are so passionate about extreme ironing that they formed a band and wrote a song about the sport entitled "Well Ironed":

"...Hey, hey you beautiful new world
    Let's call the moon a billion times a blink
    And we iron the sea until the wind tires..."

Ironists to watch: The whole team.

Paying attention to detail

GERMANY

Extreme ironing in Germany is run by the German Extreme Ironing Section, led by Hot Crease of Munich. I first met Hot Crease in New Zealand at the time of the Millennium celebrations: fascinated by extreme ironing, he took the sport back to Germany and set about encouraging its take-up.

As well as organising the first ever Extreme Ironing World Championships, the GEIS made a film about extreme ironing which was shown to a sell-out crowd at Kino24, a day-long film festival held in Munich in 2001.

A hotbed of ironing talent, The GEIS also produced the first non-powered sport irons using DSS Sorption technology, and are the brains behind the creation of both Water-style extreme ironing and Eso-Ironing.

Demonstrating "rapid ironing"

Iron Hook's laid back approach

Germany is home to the largest extreme ironing contingent outside Great Britain and the popularity of the sport is growing all the time. The German extreme ironists are highly organised and technically superb, knowing that the secret to winning competitions lies in high quality ironing.

Head of the GEIS, Hot Crease, says: "After meeting Steam in New Zealand, I was fascinated by extreme ironing. I wanted to take this crazy sport back to Germany and take on the British at their own game. Despite the surge in interest around the world, we still regard the British ironists as the best."

Ironists to watch: HGSS, Hot Pants, Iron Hook, Iron Lung.

Hot Crease, GEIS founder

GREAT BRITAIN

Having invented the sport, the British team are conscious that extreme ironing could fall the way of other British-born sports, such as cricket, football, rugby and golf – initial success followed by years of disappointment despite a nation's high expectations.

But for now, at least, the future looks bright. There is a real sense of optimism in the camp. "With success in early extreme ironing competitions, we've savoured the taste of victory and we don't want to give up that feeling," says British team ironist, Fe.

The British ironists are some of the sport's all-rounders displaying a solid ability in each of the extreme ironing disciplines – Water, Rocky, Forest, Urban and Freestyle – without specialising in any particular style. The British have a reputation on the extreme ironing circuit for fair play and teamwork.

Starch on top of his game

Ironside finds a ledge for a spot of ironing

Rivelin edge in the Peak district is an ideal training ground for extreme ironing

Sharing a heated rivalry with Germany, the British Extreme Ironing squad, with backing by sponsors Rowenta, went to the World Championships with high hopes of bringing home some silverware.

"The pleasure you get from being up a tree or on a crag somewhere with a pile of creased shirts is immense. To be able to come down from a day's adventure or activity with a load of pressed laundry – there's nothing quite like it really," says Starch, one of the top British ironists.

Ironists to watch: Fe, Ironside, Starch, Tirony.

Starch and Ironside consider the finer points

HOLLAND

The Netherlands is the latest nation to join the extreme ironing craze and has taken to the sport like starch to a collar. Extreme ironing in the Netherlands was first taken up by a team from Internet magazine NU WIJ WEER! (www.nuwijweer.nl). Since then they have appeared on Dutch television and the Dutch Extreme Ironing Section plans to hold its own event to showcase the best of Dutch talent.

The Dutch ironists show particular skill in Forest-style and Urban-style extreme ironing. No tree is too high nor any street too busy for the brave ironists, which is just as well given the lack of mountains to hone their Rocky-style moves. Dutch ironists also have an artistic flair. Coming from a country that produced Rembrandt, Vermeer and Van Gogh, you can see why.

Ironists to watch: Flat-Iron

Ironist stops traffic

A step up for extreme ironing

ICELAND

Let no one say that Icelanders don't know how to take ironing to new levels of extremity. Not content with ironing up freezing mountains, the team from Westfjords, decided to add an edge by removing a few layers of clothes.

In the country's capital, Reykjavik, geothermal energy is used to provide economical, non-polluting heating to the city's buildings. Although new to the sport, Icelanders are already at the forefront of harnessing this power, and may beat the Germans to come up with a successful "Geothermics" system.

The centre of Iceland contains stunning contrasts. It is largely an arctic desert, punctuated with mountains, glaciers, volcanoes and waterfalls – a truly ideal landscape for extreme ironing.

The country's traditional sport is glíma (Icelandic wrestling) – a unique national sport with a history dating back to the days of settlement in the 9th century. However, its dominance may be short-lived, with extreme ironing set to make use of those summer months of round-the-clock daylight.

Ironists to watch: Hot Gylfi

Ironing the shirt off your back

JAPAN

The land of the rising iron is set to be a force in extreme ironing in the near future. It is thought that a secret research and development agency led by Hithotchi is inventing the smallest, lightest, hottest iron ever seen – especially designed for extreme ironing. Up until now, examples of Japanese extreme ironing have been few and far between, but the country is increasingly looked on as a sleeping giant in the extreme ironing world.

One of my few experiences of Japanese interest in extreme ironing came when I was invited to speak on the Japanese radio station, ZIP-FM. The interviewer was so excited about the advent of this new sport that he asked me to make the "whoosh" sound of a steaming iron and promptly played Iron Maiden's "Run to the Hills".

Ironists to watch: Hithotchi, Nippon Fire.

Off-the-wall ironing

NEW ZEALAND

Not to be outdone by their Australian neighbours, New Zealand ironists are expected to make an impression on future extreme ironing competitions. Organisers of the sport in New Zealand are hoping to repeat their success in Rugby and are planning to organise a Tri-Nations Southern Hemisphere cup against Australia and South Africa.

New Zealanders are keen on outdoors sports and welcome the opportunity to take ironing and combine it with other extreme sports. In the UK, Kiwi ironists Hot Spring and Ironakka have been training with British ironists to take a few tips back to team captain Ultimate Board in time for the next World Championships.

"What a stylie sport. You have got me motivated now to try this out. Mount Cook here I come!" says Ultimate Board.

Ironists to watch: Ultimate Board.

Iron while damp

Ironakka training for the Championships

SOUTH AFRICA

A number of South African ironists entered the "Extreme Ironing Around the World" competition, where they received a number of commendations and a third place for their efforts. The daring South Africans weren't able to attend the World Championships in 2002, due to difficulties attracting sponsorship, but the nation is still expected to be a significant presence in the future.

Dironmond, a Cape Town-based ironist, is excited by the possibilities of Water-style ironing: "Now that underwater ironing has been achieved, I think the next big step is extreme ironing whilst cage diving with a great white shark. At least you'd have the iron for protection if anything went wrong!"

Ironists to watch: Nani, Pressless.

A blend of extension lead and bungee rope

UNITED STATES

There has already been a great deal of interest from the United States in hosting the World Championships. I for one am twitching my flex in anticipation of such a competition. The sheer variety and extremity of landscapes in the US will present quite a challenge.

Having already undertaken a couple of ironing sessions in New York and Colorado, Starch and I intend to return to break the American extreme sports market with an extreme ironing tour encompassing all 52 states.

Leading competitors at the moment are husband and wife team, Wash and Wear. The Colorado pair are used to ironing at altitude and have put in some decent practice moves on the Great Sand Dunes in Colorado. If they can build up a good team around them, they could challenge for the title.

Ironists to watch: Wash and Wear.

Extreme ironing US-style

PART FOUR: COMPETITION

CHAMPIONSHIP TRAINING

In June 2002, with the World Championships just around the corner, we decided that, if we we were going to compete against tournament favourites, Germany, and strive for a British victory, we needed to get in some steel-edged ironing practice.

Britain's three highest peaks were deemed an ideal training run for the World Championships, which was expected to attract entrants from a dozen countries. We might be the founding nation, but that counts for nothing in sport.

Together with the rest of the British squad our team set out to conquer Scotland's Ben Nevis (4,400 feet), England's Scafell Pike (3,210 feet), and Wales's Snowdon (3,559 feet) – taking domestic chores to new limits, along the way, by ironing selected items of laundry at the summit of each peak.

Reaching the summit

Ben Nevis provided the perfect training ground

Basket and Tirony discuss team tactics

THE THREE PEAKS

Our challenge started at 9.30am at Ben Nevis; I was sharing a board with Basket. The start of the track was pretty hard going and I wondered if we would make it. A woman stopped me and asked if I had found the ironing board at the top of the mountain. Who would leave an ironing board at the top of Ben Nevis? There's a bit of litter around the summit, but not much in the way of used household appliances.

After just over two hours we reached the top and I had time to get some wrinkles out of my scarf. As far as I am aware we were the first to iron at the top of Ben Nevis, and, although we couldn't see much through the mist, I felt a joy not matched since that first pressed shirt.

Safety Setting, the group's safety officer, warned us of the risks of exposure, and, with the weather getting colder and the mist growing heavy, we took the decision to descend.

After climbing and ironing Scafell Pike in England's Lake District, we had the long journey to Snowdon in Wales. The Crib Goch route is the most challenging of Snowdon's ascents, requiring the climber to walk across a knife-edge ridge to reach the summit. I am scared of heights, so Basket took charge of the board in the high wind. He seemed unconcerned with the height and steadied himself as the wind blew. Suddenly extreme ironing seemed a pretty stupid thing to do. Here Basket was, the ironing board strapped to his back and acting like a sail on a high mountain with a sheer drop on each side. However Basket's climbing skills (and nerve) were greater than mine, and we made it along the ridge and on to the summit for some extreme ironing.

After such rigorous training we felt ready to take on the Germans. Nothing was going to stop us winning that trophy – nothing unless it went to penalties.

WORLD CHAMPIONSHIPS

When extreme ironing first started, little thought was given to participating in the sport on a competitive basis. After all, ironists just did it for the challenge.

This all changed with the first ever Extreme Ironing World Championships, held on 21st September 2002 in Munich, Germany.

The EIB was challenged with finding a way to judge who was the best extreme ironist. The task fell to the German Extreme Ironing Section (GEIS) which was organising the event. Working closely with the EIB, the GEIS developed a scoring system that took into account speed, extreme style and, most importantly, quality of ironing.

Ironists have to get as quickly as possible around the five stations dotted along the 1-km long course, each representing one of the different extreme ironing styles: Forest, Water, Rocky, Urban and Freestyle.

Every competitor has to run (drag) their own board with them and use the pre-heated irons provided at each station. Each station has its own team of international judges to assess the the quality both of a competitor's ironing and of his or her "extreme" style. In a competitive ironing showdown, prizes are awarded for best individual ironist and best team (of three).

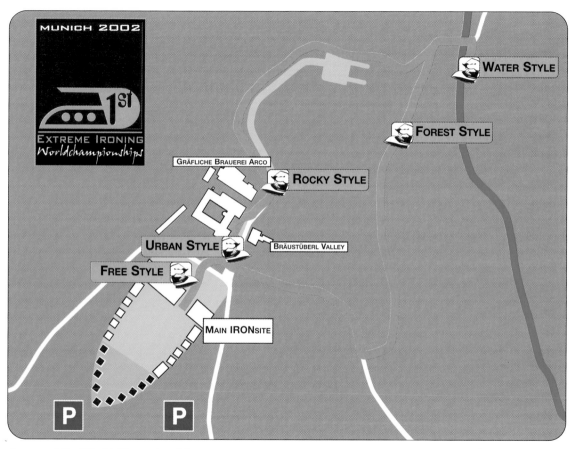

A map of the World Championships

Austrian ironist tackles the Forest section

Scoring breakdown:

- **Speed (out of 20):**
  How quickly the ironist gets around
  the course.
- **Style (out of 40):**
  How "extreme" the ironist is.
  Originality of moves.
  Difficulty of moves.
  How composed they look.
- **Ironing (out of 60)**
  How well-pressed the garment is.

Over 80 competitors from ten countries were going to be pitching themselves against each other, iron-to-iron, taking the sport to its absolute limit. In teams of three, ironists were required to run around a gruelling course, stopping at five different stations for a quick spot of ironing. It was time to find out who was top of the pile.

As captain of the British team, sponsored by Rowenta, I had some pre-competition nerves.

The other nations regarded us as one of the favourites – but I was not so sure. I had been drawn against the German favourite, Iron Hook. I'd seen pictures of him in training: he's the Michael Schumacher of extreme ironing – square-jawed, blonde, confident – I was going to have to iron the best laundry of my life to stand a chance of beating him.

"I've seen better," says one high-minded judge

An ironed shirt in hand is worth two in the basket

THE DAY OF THE CHAMPIONSHIPS

At the Forest section, the Austrians are making a name for themselves, ascending a tree with climbing spikes unaided and ironing at the top. Another irons upside down. Luckily for us, Starch has practised that manoeuvre and puts in a crisp performance.

Since yesterday's downpour, the river is flowing fast at the Water section. The Germans are doing well, mastering the use of canoes and surfboards while ironing. Other ironists are brave enough to enter the water naked. I opt for the rubber ring, don my goggles, pick up my cordless iron and head upstream. To rally the team I sing the British National Anthem; the combination of ironing and national pride goes down well with the crowds.

At the Rocky section's high, purpose-built climbing wall, a large crowd gathers. Most of the competitors put in good performances – particularly the Polish and Italians. The judges

Iron Hook makes a monkey of the opposition

have a difficult job picking who is the best. Our very own Lazer puts in an assured (inverted) performance and Hotplate impresses the judges enough to get maximum points.

A wrecked car is the main prop at the Urban station. Here, ironists display real imagination, climbing on the roof, inside, underneath and hanging off doors. German competitor, Hot Pants, turns up on a bicycle and her compatriot Iron Mike manages to fall through the window – thankfully he only suffers cuts and bruises. In the British camp, the cameras seem strangely fixated by the sight of Iron Matron ironing on the car's back seat.

The final section is the Freestyle event and things are really hotting up. Here competitors can do what they like and ironists are out to impress again. The first to reach this section is High Grade Steel Sole, who wows the judges with his kick-ironing – attaching the hot iron to his foot. Iron Mike impresses judges with his

ironing and trampolining skills, while another German ironist turns up ironing on the back of a motorised scooter. The highly-organised Germans and daring Austrians are looking favourites for the medals.

With the events all over, competitors wait expectantly for the results, like the end of a spin-cycle. In the team event the British team GB3 get bronze, while the top German team win silver. My own team, GB1, with Basket and Starch comes away with gold! In the individual event, German ironist Hot Pants scoops top honours, winning a trip to Hawaii. It has been a fantastic event, with a few surprises in the results which will be discussed all night long. I congratulate Iron Hook on his efforts – he'd come fourth, with his team managing silver. For my part, I am still getting to grips with being part of the best extreme ironing team in the world.

Points were awarded for speed, style and quality of ironing

First: Troye Wallett, Wolfberg Cracks, South Africa (Picture taken by Gordon Forbes, South Africa)

ROWENTA TROPHY 2003

In February 2003 the Extreme Ironing Bureau launched the Rowenta Trophy – a worldwide competition to find out who could take ironing to its most extreme levels yet. Following the success of the 2001 picture competition and 2002 World Championships, the EIB cast its net wider than ever before in search of the perfect press. Competitors were asked to submit pictures of ironing in the most bizarre, unusual, amusing and extreme places. As usual, judging was a challenge, but I hope you agree that these are some of the best examples of extreme ironing yet.

Second: Robert Fry, The Blue Mountains, Australia
(Picture taken by Simon Plum, Australia)

Cool Silk, one of the ten-strong judging panel, said, "From the 160 or so entries we had this year, judging was more difficult than ever. Spare a thought for ironists Ben Gibbons and John Roberts who took their iron and board above Base Camp One on Mount Everest and only managed eighth place. Their laundry didn't stack up against a South African imitating clothes hanging out to dry across a gorge, an Australian with parachute and a Brit ironing at the centre of the Earth."

Third: Adi Hooper, Alum Pot, UK
(Picture taken by Hugh Penney, UK)

Fourth: Kim Clark (UK), The Alps, France
(Picture taken by Dave Evans, UK)

Fifth: Mattieu de Villiers, The Maltese Cross, S. Africa
(Picture taken by Gordon Forbes, South Africa)

THE FUTURE...

In 1997, extreme ironing was practised by just two people, Spray and me. Now, hundreds of people are taking their ironing outdoors, with numbers swelling all the time.

Some people ask me whether extreme ironing will spawn a whole host of other extreme sports based upon household chores such as vacuum cleaning. But to me, this seems entirely pointless. You are no more likely to see me jousting with a mop or vacuuming outdoors than to find out that I've taken up learning to juggle with bananas. For me, the purest and only form of white goods extreme sport is extreme ironing.

I believe that the future is bright for extreme ironing. In its next stage of development we expect the sport to turn professional and, who knows, one day appear in the Olympics. For those doubters out there, I have two words to say to you: synchronised swimming!

Everest, Base Camp One. How long before extreme ironing reaches the summit?

GETTING IN TOUCH

For more information, visit the EIB's website www.extremeironing.com. Visitors can join the worldwide extreme ironing community, submit pictures, join online forums and visit other extreme ironing websites. Contact the EIB direct by emailing: info@extremeironing.com.

Iron on!
Steam

ACKNOWLEDGEMENTS

Both this book and the growth of extreme ironing couldn't have been achieved without the help and support of a number of people.
Special thanks to:
Austrian Extreme Ironing Section, Dash (Proctor & Gamble), Melanie Katchinski and the MSLPR team, Rowenta, and Kai Zosseder and the GEIS.
Thanks also to:
Claire Agnew, Eliya Armen, Kasia Baldwin, Paul Cartwright, Julie Darroch, Martin Durkin and the WagTV team, Dave Fitzgerald, Steve Green, Jo Hare, Steve Harrison, James Ireson, David Jeanson, Emma Johns, Karen Kelly, Tristan Kitchener, Kim Kremer, Elaine Law, Ute Mayer, Richard Park, Roger Prince, Helen Reeve, Sarah Scovell, Patrick Semple, Joe Sterling, and, of course, my mum for teaching me how to iron in the first place.

The Extreme Ironing Bureau is led by Matthew Scull (Starch) and Phil Shaw (Steam).

PHOTOGRAPHY

Kevin M Beck: pp 37t
Sven Bratulic, Dash: pp 66–7; 69
Simon Buckley: pp 40
Paul Cartwright: pp 8
Club "Extremkunstsport e.V.": pp 14r; 15; 18; 29; 38; 57l; 61; 76; 87
Leendert Douma: pp 74t; 74b
Dave Evans pp 94bl
Norbert Fuchs: Back cover – l & ml; pp 7; 23; 24–5; 28; 30–31; 62–3
Ben Gibbons/John Roberts – pp 95
Birgir Thór Halldórsson: Back cover – mr; pp 75
Bernd Hau, Dash: pp 39; 41; 86; 89; 91
EIB (Kasia Baldwin; Julie Darroch; Steve Harrison; James Ireson; Emma Johns; Elaine Law; Matthew Scull; Phil Shaw; Penny Wilkinson): pp 2; 9; 11; 12; 13; 14l; 16l; 16r; 20; 21; 32b; 42; 43; 45r; 46; 47; 48; 49; 50; 51; 54; 55; 58; 59b; 70; 71; 72; 73; 77t; 77b; 79; 80; 81; 82; 88
Gordon Forbes: pp 78; 92; 94r
James Howe: pp 19
Karen Kelly/Kim Kremer: pp 44; 45l
Christian Krinninger: pp 56; 57r
Pablo Andres Letelier Meza: pp 64
Ian Mitchell: pp 36t; 36b; 37b
Peter Musch, Dash: pp 26–7; 68
Hugh Penney pp 94tl
Simon Plum pp 93
Craig Simons: pp 22; 32t; 60
Schalchi: Back cover – r; pp 34; 35t; 35b; 59 b
Sarah Scovell: pp 10; 33; 65
BJ Stevens: pp 52; 53t; 53b

LOGO DESIGN

coma ag (World Champs logos & map): 84–85
Jo Hare (Extreme Ironing logo): Front cover; Spine; pp 1; 3
Rowenta (Rowenta Trophy logo): pp 92